EARLY BIRD ON SESAME STREET

By Linda Hayward
Illustrated by Tom Leigh

A SESAME STREET/GOLDEN PRESS BOOK

Published by Western Publishing Company, Inc.,
in conjunction with Children's Television Workshop.

It was early morning on Sesame Street.

The sky was still dark.

Everyone was still asleep.

Everyone, that is, except Big Bird.
Big Bird was wide awake.
He sat up in his nest and listened.

He got up and looked around.
There was no one to play with.
"Where is everybody?" Big Bird asked. He began to walk.
"I'll walk until I find someone to play with," he said.

Big Bird walked up the street and around the corner.
When he came to a bakery, he stopped.
Inside the bakery the bakers were taking loaves of
bread out of the oven.
"Everyone there is too busy to play," said Big Bird.
So he went on walking.

When he came to a fruit and vegetable market, he stopped.
Outside the market the fruit and vegetable sellers were
taking boxes of fruits and vegetables off a truck.
"Everyone here is too busy to play," said Big Bird.
He went on walking.

Big Bird stopped at a firehouse. The fire fighters
were washing the fire engine.
"Everyone here is busy, too," Big Bird said, sighing.
So he went on walking.

Big Bird came to a police station and stopped.

The police officers were standing in a straight line for inspection.
"Oh, dear. Everyone is busy this morning," said Big Bird.
And he went on walking.

At the newspaper stand, the seller was untying
bundles of newspapers.
"She looks too busy to play," said Big Bird.
So he went on walking.

Soon Big Bird came to a window with clocks
in it.

All the clocks said seven o'clock.

"Seven o'clock?" said Big Bird with surprise. "That's
the time I usually get up in the morning. I must be an
early bird today."

Big Bird walked back to Sesame Street.
By the time he got home he was very tired.
"I think I will take a little nap," said Big Bird.

Meanwhile, all of Big Bird's friends were waking up.

Betty Lou was making her bed.

The Count was brushing his teeth.

Cookie Monster was brushing his fur.

Oscar was reading the *Grouch Gazette*.

Bert and Ernie were eating breakfast.

Little Bird was washing his face.

Sherlock Hemlock was adjusting his hat.
Everyone was busy at the start of a new day.

Everyone, that is, except Big Bird.
"Wake up, sleepyhead!" said Little Bird.
"It's time to get up!"
But Big Bird was fast asleep.